SIGNS & SKY-MATES

ASTROLOGICAL COMPATIBILITY DECK

Dossé-Via Trenou

T0364053

RP Minis®
Hachette Book Group
1290 Avenue of the Americas, New York, NY 10104
www.runningpress.com
@Running_Press

First edition: December 2022

Published by RP Minis, an imprint of Perseus Books,
LLC, a subsidiary of Hachette Book Group, Inc. The RP
Minis name and logo is a registered trademark of the
Hachette Book Group.

The Hachette Speakers Bureau provides a wide range
of authors for speaking events. To find out more, go to
www.hachettespeakersbureau.com or call (866) 376-6591.

The publisher is not responsible for websites (or their
content) that are not owned by the publisher.

ISBN: 978-0-7624-7802-6

Contents

Introduction

Let me tell you a secret: The Universe wants you to feel love. It wants you to experience rich friendships. And it wants you to excel in whatever you decide to pursue. The Universe wants you to feel sexual bliss and intellectual stimulation. It wants you to travel, learn, teach, remember.

The Universe wants you to see yourself reflected within it. It's here to help you create a life you feel compatible with while meeting and merging with those with whom you're most in tune. You've probably asked yourself the question, *What people am I compatible with and how can I find them?* These cards and this booklet will help you answer that question.

How the Cards Work

* When you have a question about a relationship—whether it's with yourself or another person, or just relationships in general—turn to the cards in this deck. Shuffle the cards while pondering your question. Let the cards search for the answer.

✳ **Draw one card at random.**

✳ **If you drew a Sign card, turn to page 13. Maybe you need more of that sign's energy in your life, whether that's through embodying more of those qualities within yourself or seeking them out in others. Alternatively, that sign could represent a core element of your own chart that you should continue to nurture or dive into more deeply. If you drew a Skymates card, turn to** page 27. Perhaps there is something about the energy of this particular pairing that could be useful to you. Maybe you'd benefit from better harmonizing or integrating those signs' energies into your chart or your life. Lean on your intuition and mystical interpretation to consider what insights the card could be offering. If you drew a Planet card, turn to page 77. Look at where that planet shows up in your natal chart, and learn from that planetary placement as you navigate whatever themes your question brings up. You can calculate your birth chart using the calculator available at KnowTheZodiac.com.

* For however long feels right to you, keep the cards nearby and continue contemplating what they could mean for you. Let your Orí lead the way.

THE
SIGNS

Aries

While Aries has often been defined as a vibrant, bold, and competitive being, there is a sensitivity and even a shyness that most Aries initially exhibit. It's as you get to know them that their wilder, more ferocious personalities truly emerge.

Taurus

Taurus has the ability to change,
evolve, and transform—but only
on their own terms, and only when
they truly want to. No one can force
them to change.

Gemini

Most Geminis appear to be younger even as they age—especially in spirit. As they cultivate wisdom, their simplicity and serenity also grow.

Cancer

Cancer's intuitive and psychic nature always allows them to do most of their work in a subconscious, behind-the-scenes way. Their thoughts and words are spells, and they're very much aware of it.

Leo

A heart-centered being—that's Leo energy. Leos, like their ruling Sun, are deeply generous, emanating rays of optimism and joy.

Virgo

Life is not as effortless for Virgos
as they make it appear. And one of
their simplest wishes is that more
people would notice that and see the
true complexity of their nature.

Libra

Libra represents the give-and-take of energy in a way that encourages harmony, reciprocity, and flow. It's about mastering what goes out and comes in and trusting that even if we're not fully sure what we're putting out, what returns to us will serve our growth in some way.

♏ Scorpio

Scorpio is the zodiac's most mysterious, alluring, vigilant, and complex sign. They are undeniably perceptive, calculating, and intrigued by the transformative world in which they live.

Sagittarius

Sagittarius has bewildering, enticing, and contagious energy. They're able to let their curiosity lead the way and also tap into the curiosity of others through their inquisitiveness.

Capricorn

Capricorns remind us that with
enough persistence and patience,
we can accomplish anything we set
our minds to. Symbolized by the goat
that slowly but surely makes its way
to the top of the mountain, no zodiac
sign has as much perseverance and
ambition as a Capricorn.

Aquarius

Not ones to stick with the status quo, Aquarians are known for paving their own path and resisting authority. They don't mind following the rules as long as the rules make sense to them.

Pisces

Pisces is represented by two fish, alluding to its ever-changing modality. A mermaid who longs not only to experience life on land, but also to bring those on land back into the water—that's Pisces energy.

THE SKY-MATES

Aries & Aries

When Aries-dominant beings connect, it's either the perfect temperature or way too hot to handle. But even if it's the latter, two Aries are bound to find a way to make an adventure out of the chaos.

Aries & Taurus

This is not the most traditional of partnerships due to these skymates' striking differences. Taurus seeks practicality and simplicity, and

Aries is born with striking passion and a desire for adventure.

Aries & Gemini

Aries and Gemini energy tends to be harmonious, but only if they have the patience to resist making assumptions about each other.

Aries & Cancer

Often friendship is the foundation of this connection first and foremost. At their best, Aries and Cancer come

together to learn how to harmonize
Aries' need for dynamic energy and
Cancer's desire for emotional security.

Aries & Leo

When the first and second Fire
signs of the zodiac come together,
they may feel like they've known
each other for a lifetime—or even
have been connected in previous
lifetimes. Passion, intensity, and
adventure characterize this union,
as do power struggles and pride.

Aries & Virgo

This pairing is likely to be drawn into a world they don't fully understand but to which they're willing to learn to adapt. Both skymates will grow when they decide to explore unknown parts within their own nature.

Aries & Libra

When Aries and Libra connect with each other as astrological opposites, they've found a cosmic counterpart who acts like a mirror, showing them the qualities and energies that exist within them but are expressed in opposing ways. Aries seeks stimulation, and Libra seeks harmony.

Aries & Scorpio

At first glance, these skymates may appear to be worlds apart. However, these signs actually have an inherently similar nature due to the fact that they share a common planetary ruler: Mars, the warrior.

Aries & Sagittarius

When the first and last Fire signs of
the zodiac conjoin, life feels like a
nonstop fireworks show—which can
be super exciting at first but may
soon become overwhelming to the
point of desensitization.

Aries & Capricorn

When these bosses come together,
their focus should be on looking
past what probably initially brought
them together—their amazing

prowess and ambition—and tapping
into the more unlikely aspects of
their emotional connection.

Aries & Aquarius

One of the defining qualities of this
pairing is an ability to keep it real
within the relationship. This allows
them to stay true to themselves
without feeling the pressure
to conform.

Aries & Pisces

The fusion of Aries and Pisces energy feels like a playground that keeps expanding from day to day. Their energy is mutually motivating, imaginative, creative, and pure.

Taurus & Taurus

Taurus-dominant beings in a relationship of any kind are intense, stubborn, and inflexible but also profoundly creative, passionate, loyal, and vigorous. They may be obsessed with each other or unable to stand each other.

Taurus & Gemini

Taurus may initially appear clingy or possessive of Gemini, but as time passes, it could be Gemini who can't get enough of Taurus.

Taurus & Cancer

There's natural harmony between these signs, even if it takes time for them to see how much their energies align. These skymates are filled with love, sensitivity, and mutual respect.

Taurus & Leo

When Taurus and Leo connect, it's a blend of Fixed Earth and Fixed Fire, meaning they are a force to be reckoned with. They're drawn to each other's strong, captivating auras.

Taurus & Virgo

Taurus and Virgo are Earth signs that thrive when they stay

connected to their roots, their values, and their senses. They're here to learn how to take themselves, and life, less seriously as a cosmic duo.

Taurus & Libra

Taurus and Libra know how to use their words and actions to make their counterpart feel loved and appreciated. Their intention is to live a pleasurable, chill life.

Taurus & Scorpio

We have all heard the phrase "opposites attract," but Scorpio and Taurus truly bring that phrase to life. This passionate and extreme duo is brought together to balance each other out.

Taurus & Sagittarius

When these skymates conjoin, it can either be a phenomenal experience or crash and burn as quickly as it began. Their mission is

to learn how to harmonize with
each other more than they disrupt
each other's flow.

Taurus &
Capricorn

"Big abundance energy" is what
comes to mind when these resilient
beings combine. They have the
ultimate luxurious vibe.

Taurus & Aquarius

Both signs are Fixed and stubborn,
so they must be on the same page
about wanting to explore each other's
depths and eccentricities. If they're
not, they'll run in opposite directions.

Taurus & Pisces

Taurus and Pisces have a deeply
comforting and healing aura about
them when they conjoin—but only if
both skymates are mature enough to
realize the blessing that is their union.

Gemini & Gemini

Two Geminis in a relationship are more like four Geminis in a relationship, and it's always hilarious trying to figure out who's in charge. The truth is, no one is.

Gemini & Cancer

When Cancer and Gemini connect with each other, they'd benefit from surrendering to the unknown and allowing their blend of spontaneity and sensitivity to guide them.

Gemini & Leo

When Gemini and Leo forge a cosmic connection, everyone wants to know how they do it. Together they come off as a confident, exciting, and youthful pair on the search for an adventure.

Gemini & Virgo

What happens when two Mercury-ruled beings connect? Anything, nothing, and everything. It depends on how much patience they have

with each other. These skymates
are both ruled by Mercury and
express Mercury's qualities in
contrasting ways.

Gemini & Libra

Gemini and Libra's love can be out
of this world. Space and a healthy
amount of emotional detachment,
as well as honest self-reflection,
are highlights of mature
Gemini-Libra duos.

Gemini & Scorpio

The word *typhoon* might bring disaster to mind, but in essence it's just the forceful combination of Air and Water turning their mutual energy into a concentrated force.

Gemini & Sagittarius

When these opposite zodiac signs connect, they give off big firefly energy. They know how to light each other up while lighting up the world simultaneously.

Gemini & Capricorn

When they move with intention,
Mutable Air and Cardinal Earth
can truly make magic happen. But
they have to accept that "moving
with intention" can mean different
things to different people.

Gemini & Aquarius

When the Mutable Gemini and
Fixed Aquarius come together,
they appreciate the versatility,
adaptability, and free-spirited

nature that their common element of Air facilitates between them. They encourage each other to grow beyond the confines of social limitations.

Gemini & Pisces

When Gemini and Pisces connect, there's an instant, unexpected synergy, and it has a calming influence on anyone in their presence.

Cancer & Cancer

When two Cancers merge, there's a telepathic connection that either makes them feel at home with each other or like there's too much merging happening at once.

Cancer & Leo

When the Moon-ruled Cancer connects with the Sun-ruled Leo, two beings who shine in different ways learn how to support each other's light without eclipsing each other's energy.

Cancer & Virgo

This connection feels like a meeting of old souls who constantly find their way back to each other. At their best, Cancer and Virgo are the epitome of Mother Nature's influence.

Cancer & Libra

This Water-Air combination has the potential to take both skymates out of their comfort zones. Still, they have a natural affinity for each other

that enables them to
communicate nonverbally.

Cancer & Scorpio

Scorpio and Cancer are the two
Water signs of the zodiac that most
resemble each other. These beings
are likely to be lifelong friends,
often tending to each other's
unspoken needs and desires.

Cancer & Sagittarius

Cancer loves Sag's larger-than-life demeanor even if Cancer would rather live in their more mellow world. Sag feels comforted watching Cancer live a more leisurely lifestyle.

Cancer & Capricorn

Opposites in the zodiac, Cancer and Capricorn complement and frustrate each other in equal measure.

Cancer & Aquarius

These signs express their deep emotions in vastly different ways. When they don't align on an idea or mission, catastrophe can ensue.

Cancer & Pisces

These Water sign beings have a spirit of ease, adaptability, and mutual love for each other but could fall prey to unhealthy codependency.

Leo & Leo

A relationship between two Leos is filled with unpredictability. When Leo skymates connect, they understand that beneath their sunny exterior, gloomier weather sometimes lingers.

Leo & Virgo

The best thing for these skymates to do is release the assumptions that they may have of each other. There's so much that Leo and Virgo are meant to learn together.

Leo & Libra

Leo and Libra give off "two peas in a pod" vibes. Their artsy and jovial natures light up their environments and remind others to enjoy the process just as much as the result.

Leo & Scorpio

They walk into the room hand in hand, fierce. They are the ultimate power couple, making people wonder where they get all their energy and confidence.

Leo & Sagittarius

In a secure relationship, Leo and Sag can be the best of friends, going on wild adventures. But if these Fire signs haven't dealt with their demons, they may get scorched by each other's flames.

Leo & Capricorn

Love them or hate them, when Leo and Capricorn get together, they're shaking tables and drawing attention. Their combined energy generates power without their even trying.

Leo & Aquarius

When these cosmic opposites connect, they may feel a fresh sense of fellowship that's not as easily found with other skymates. They give the impression that there is always a running joke between them even if all they do is exchange eye contact and burst into laughter.

Leo & Pisces

When Fixed Fire and Mutable
Water engage in a relationship,
no one knows what to expect.
Every moment feels like a
chance for reinvention.

Virgo & Virgo

These skymates are humble
geniuses who often go unnoticed
up until the moment they decide
to give themselves the credit they
deserve. Once they do, it's a wrap.

Virgo & Libra

Virgo and Libra may appear to be an odd match, but the more patient they are in the process of uncovering each other's mysteries, the more riveting their connection becomes. They are drawn to the qualities that they feel are missing in themselves.

Virgo & Scorpio

In the beginning, neither sign will want to admit their desire to be with the other. Both are used to keeping their distance until the ice has been broken.

Virgo & Sagittarius

Finding some sort of equilibrium between the deep sensitivity inherent in Virgo and the wild unpredictability inherent in Sagittarius is key to these signs' existing in harmony.

Virgo & Capricorn

These skymates know that great
things take time, so they're willing
to invest in their partnership
by trusting that what's meant
to be will be.

Virgo & Aquarius

Virgo and Aquarius mobilize each
other to be more curious about
each other's differences rather than
turned off by them. They hold each
other accountable.

Virgo & Pisces

When the cosmic opposites Virgo and Pisces conjoin, Virgo should do their best not to judge Pisces's existential nature. Pisces should do their best not to assume that Virgo is boring.

Libra & Libra

When these skymates conjoin, they feel energized by their ability to talk about anything under the Sun. They may question each other's motives because they know each other so well.

Libra & Scorpio

In many ways, the facts that Scorpio follows Libra in the sequence of zodiac signs and that both are uniquely focused on partnership make it seem like these signs complete one another.

Libra & Sagittarius

These skymates know how to keep the party going, and going, and going. But what happens when it stops? The party revives itself, of course. At times this duo forgets how to slow down.

Libra & Capricorn

When Libra and Capricorn energies merge, it can feel like both a settled vibration and a breath of fresh air. Libra helps Capricorn have fun and release their stressors. Capricorn brings responsibility and stability to Libra's versatile lifestyle.

Libra & Aquarius

These Air signs must accept the impermanence of their connection and trust that even if they occasionally drift apart, the essence of their synergy will remain with them in some form.

Libra & Pisces

Libra and Pisces experience several flashes of insight when they're together, to the point where it almost feels destined for them to meet. They can easily become each other's muses.

Scorpio & Scorpio

This is a relationship that obsesses, consumes, and transforms everything around it—especially the two individuals in question. Even if it begins on what appears to be a lighthearted note, it has a hidden, deeper foundation.

Scorpio & Sagittarius

Scorpio, being the dark, brooding mystery, intrigues the lighthearted and impulsive Sagittarius. Sagittarius is equally compelling to the more reserved and cautious Scorpio.

Scorpio & Capricorn

Scorpio and Capricorn command authority with every bold, precise, and well-calculated move they make. It is no wonder they are drawn to each other's energies,

although neither sign will want
to make the first move.

Scorpio & Aquarius

These Fixed signs live by their own
rules and set their own standards.
Their resistance to authority is a
big reason they are able to begin a
relationship in the first place.

Scorpio & Pisces

Traditionally known as the soulmates
of the zodiac, Scorpio and Pisces

mesh like two mystical sea creatures destined to meet. Scorpio always knows how Pisces feels, while Pisces knows who Scorpio truly wants to be.

Sagittarius & Sagittarius

These Jupiter-ruled skymates can be pretty calm and mellow, while at the same time they're able to spring into spontaneous action. They are curious about the world and about what lies within.

Sagittarius & Capricorn

Sagittarius is more than a jokester, and Capricorn is more than a workaholic. It's when they take time to step out of these roles that they're able to recognize each other's multitudes.

Sagittarius & Aquarius

Judged as carefree and heartless, these skymates are actually quite in tune with the depths of humanity, choosing to experience life in multiple dimensions and from varied perspectives.

Sagittarius & Pisces

The idealists and dreamers of the zodiac, these signs struggle when it comes to following through. It's their ability to make a big deal out of things, or to let them go, that keeps this connection refreshing and unpredictable.

Capricorn & Capricorn

Capricorns together are filled with major powerhouse vibes. These skymates feel like they've met someone who understands why they tend to take life so seriously.

Capricorn & Aquarius

When the individualistic and responsible Capricorn connects with the rebellious and unconventional Aquarius, both signs learn how to deepen their trust for each other, even if that means stepping out of their comfort zones.

Capricorn & Pisces

When Capricorn and Pisces connect, the fusion of Earth and Water feels nurturing and healing for both skymates.

Aquarius & Aquarius

When Aquarius meets Aquarius, even though their ideologies and philosophies may be completely different, they both feel at ease knowing that their ideas won't be seen as too "out there."

Aquarius & Pisces

These skymates invite each other into their worlds. They understand that life is more fun when they experience it together rather than apart.

Pisces & Pisces

Pisces skymates connect to remind the world that slowing down, closing our eyes, and snuggling together are ways of life.

THE
PLANETS

The Sun

The Sun's placement in our chart shows how our central energy is expressed or has the potential to be expressed. It exposes our essence and highlights both our strengths and areas where we can improve.

The Moon

The Moon's wisdom is healing, freeing us as we allow ourselves to feel the total range of our emotions. It doesn't ask us to compartmentalize these feelings—instead the Moon teaches us that everything we feel is useful, especially the emotions we try to discard.

Mercury

In Yorùbá spirituality, Mercury
is represented by Èṣù, Ọlọrun's
linguist. He's known as the master of
languages—a trickster. The guru of
both communication and crossroads,
Èṣù is called on to deepen our verbal
and nonverbal gifts as we quickly
solve problems using the power of
thought, intention, and intellect.

Venus

Venus guides us toward knowing how to be in relationship with ourselves, others, animals, our consciousness, our material world, and the things we may not see. It is the planet of magnetism and social connection. It helps us attract money, beauty, luxury, wealth, abundance, and, at times, frivolity, overindulgence, jealousy, possessiveness, and passion.

Mars

Mars shows us what we'd be doing if we'd just let ourselves. It also shows us what we're afraid to do, even if we know that doing so would unlock another level of potential. Our Mars sign represents the initiative, or lack thereof, we may have in life. It shows us how we assert ourselves or how we don't.

Jupiter

We are Jupiter's disciples as we explore what abundance truly means and cultivate our own forms of knowledge, spiritual initiations, and luck through the process of being alive and curious about what life means. Jupiter is not only about what life brings to us, but also what we pour into life.

Saturn

Saturn ensures that each human faces the trials they need to grow. It's not up to other humans to decide which growth is the most authentic or the most valuable. We all grow differently. Focus on your own growth, adhere to your own path, put in your own work, and you will see progress.

Uranus

Uranus sparks change in unexpected ways, reminding us that change is the only constant in life. Uranus has the type of energy that makes us talk about things others may prefer to brush under the rug.

Neptune

Neptune encourages us to dive
within our own subconscious in
a way that feels so familiar we
eventually can't tell the difference
between our conscious and
our subconscious.

Pluto

Pluto teaches us not to fear our own destruction. Instead, we should view it as a natural process of life, like birth. Are you willing to do the work to rebuild yourself and your spiritual foundations whenever the time for rebirth comes?

This book has been bound using
handcraft methods and Smyth-sewn
to ensure durability.

—※—

Illustrated by Neka King
Designed by Susan Van Horn

ALSO AVAILABLE

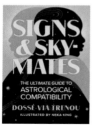